D1544307

Saint Judas

They answered

and said unto him,

Thou wast altogether born in sin,

and dost thou teach us?

And they

cast him out

Saint Judas

by James Wright

Wesleyan University Press
Middletown, Connecticut

For permission to reprint some of these poems, the author wishes to thank the editors of the following: *The Hudson Review, The Kenyon Review, The Sewanee Review, The Western Review, The Yale Review, Best Articles and Stories, Harper's Magazine, The New Orleans Poetry Journal, Poetry: a Magazine of Verse, The University of Connecticut Fine Arts Magazine, Frescoe, The New Poets of England and America, The Paris Review, The Guinness Book of Poetry, The London Magazine, Assay,* and *Botteghe Oscure.* The poems "What the Earth Asked Me" and "Evening" appeared originally in *The New Yorker.* Thanks are due also to Mr. John Crowe Ransom and his associates for the Kenyon Review Fellowship in Poetry (1958), which made possible the completion of this book.

Library of Congress Catalog Card Number: 59–12481
Manufactured in the United States of America

to Philip Timberlake, my teacher
and to Sonjia Urseth, my student

*I stop my habitual thinking, as if the plow had
suddenly run deeper in its furrow through the
crust of the world. How can I go on, who have just
stepped over such a bottomless skylight in the bog
of my life? Suddenly old Time winked at me,—Ah you
know me, you rogue,—and news had come that IT was
well. . . . Heal yourselves, doctors; by God I live.*
—THOREAU, A Week on the
Concord and Merrimack Rivers

Contents

II. A Sequence of Love Poems

III. The Part Nearest Home

I. Lunar Changes

Complaint

She's gone. She was my love, my moon or more.
She chased the chickens out and swept the floor,
Emptied the bones and nut-shells after feasts,
And smacked the kids for leaping up like beasts.
Now morbid boys have grown past awkwardness;
The girls let stitches out, dress after dress,
To free some swinging body's riding space
And form the new child's unimagined face.
Yet, while vague nephews, spitting on their curls,
Amble to pester winds and blowsy girls,
What arm will sweep the room, what hand will hold
New snow against the milk to keep it cold?
And who will dump the garbage, feed the hogs,
And pitch the chickens' heads to hungry dogs?
Not my lost hag who dumbly bore such pain:
Childbirth and midnight sassafras and rain.
New snow against her face and hands she bore,
And now lies down, who was my moon or more.

I used to see her in the door,
Lifting up her hand to wave
To citizens, or pass the hour
With neighboring wives who did not have
Anything more than time to say.

I used to see her in the door,
Simple and quiet woman, slim;
And so, I think, Paul cared the more
The night they carried her from him,
The night they carried her away.

The doctor did not even ask
For any neighborly advice;
He knew he had a simple task,
And it was obvious from his eyes
There was not anything to say.

The doctor had a word for Paul;
He said that she was resting now,
And would not wake, and that was all.
And then he walked into the snow,
Into the snow he walked away.

And did Paul shriek and curse the air,
And did he pummel with his fist
Against the wall, or tear his hair
And rush outside to bite the mist
That did not have a thing to say?

He sat upon her ruffled bed
And did not even look at me.
She was lovely, she was dead.
Some sparrows chirruped on a tree
Outside, and then they flew away.

An Offering for Mr. Bluehart

That was a place, when I was young,
Where two or three good friends and I
Tested the fruit against the tongue
Or threw the withered windfalls by.
The sparrows, angry in the sky,
Denounced us from a broken bough.
They limp along the wind and die.
The apples all are eaten now.

Behind the orchard, past one hill
The lean satanic owner lay
And threatened us with murder till
We stole his riches all away.
He caught us in the act one day
And damned us to the laughing bone,
And fired his gun across the gray
Autumn where now his life is done.

Sorry for him, or any man
Who lost his labored wealth to thieves,
Today I mourn him, as I can,
By leaving in their golden leaves
Some luscious apples overhead.
Now may my abstinence restore
Peace to the orchard and the dead.
We shall not nag them any more.

He sits before me now, reptilian, cold,
Worn skeletal with sorrow for his child.
He would have lied to her, were he not old:
An old man's fumbling lips are not defiled
By the sweet lies of love. Yet one must be
Skillful to bring it off; that treachery
Whips back to lash the bungler of its art.
He curses his ineptitude of heart.

He knows the quivering eye of youth is blind.
The pale ears, roaring deep as shell, are deaf
To the half-drowning cry of love behind
The skull. His daughter struck him in her grief
Across the face, hearing her lover dead.
He stood behind her chair, he bowed his head,
Knowing that even death cannot prolong
The quick hysteric angers of the young.

I can say nothing. I will see him sit
Under the vacant clock, till I grow old.
The barkeep's wife returns to throw her fit
And pitch us out into the early cold.
I touch his shoulder, but he does not move,
Lost in the blind bewilderment of love,
The meaningless despair that could not keep
His daughter long from falling off to sleep.

Meanwhile, the many faces of old age
Flutter before me in the tavern haze.
He cannot let me see him weep and rage
Into his wrinkled pillow. Face by face,

He grins to entertain, he fills my glass,
Cold to the gestures of my vague *alas*,
Gay as a futile god who cannot die
Till daylight, when the barkeep says goodbye.

Pitiful dupes of old illusion, lost
And fallen in the white, they glitter still
Sprightly as when they bathed in summer dust,
Then fade among the crystals on the hill.

Lonely for warm days when the season broke,
Alert to wing and fire, they must have flown
To rest among those toughened boughs of oak
That brood above us, now the fire is gone.

Walking around to breathe, I kick aside
The soft brown feather and the brittle beak.
All flesh is fallen snow. The days deride
The wings of these deluded, once they break.

Somewhere the race of wittier birds survive,
Southering slowly with the cooling days.
They pause to quiver in the wind alive
Like some secure felicity of phrase.

But these few blunderers below my hands
Assault the ear with silence on the wind.
I lose their words, though winter understands.
Man is the listener gone deaf and blind.

The oak above us shivers in the bleak
And lucid winter day; and, far below
Our gathering of the cheated and the weak,
A chimney whispers to a cloud of snow.

A Note Left in Jimmy Leonard's Shack

Near the dry river's water-mark we found
    Your brother Minnegan,
Flopped like a fish against the muddy ground.
Beany, the kid whose yellow hair turns green,
Told me to find you, even in the rain,
    And tell you he was drowned.

I hid behind the chassis on the bank,
    The wreck of someone's Ford:
I was afraid to come and wake you drunk:
You told me once the waking up was hard,
The daylight beating at you like a board.
    Blood in my stomach sank.

Besides, you told him never to go out
    Along the river-side
Drinking and singing, clattering about.
You might have thrown a rock at me and cried
I was to blame, I let him fall in the road
    And pitch down on his side.

Well, I'll get hell enough when I get home
    For coming up this far,
Leaving the note, and running as I came.
I'll go and tell my father where you are.
You'd better go find Minnegan before
    Policemen hear and come.

Beany went home, and I got sick and ran,
    You old son of a bitch.
You better hurry down to Minnegan;
He's drunk or dying now, I don't know which,
Rolled in the roots and garbage like a fish,
    The poor old man.

1

The nurse carried him up the stair
Into his mother's sleeping room.
The beeches lashed the roof and dragged the air
 Because of storm.

Wind could have overturned the dead.
Moth and beetle and housefly crept
Under the door to find the lamp, and cowered:
 But still he slept.

The ache and sorrow of darkened earth
Left pathways soft and meadows sodden;
The small Frome overflowed the firth,
 And he lay hidden

In the arms of the tall woman gone
To soothe his mother during the dark;
Nestled against the awkward flesh and bone
 When the rain broke.

2

Last night at Stinsford where his heart
Is buried now, the rain came down.
Cold to the hidden joy, the secret hurt,
 His heart is stone.

But over the dead leaves in the wet
The mouse goes snooping, and the bird.
Something the voiceless earth does not forget
 They come to guard,

Maybe, the heart who would not tell
Whatever secret he learned from the ground,
Who turned aside and heard the human wail,
    That other sound.

More likely, though, the laboring feet
Of fieldmouse, hedgehog, moth and hawk
Seek in the storm what comfort they can get
    Under the rock

Where surely the heart will not wake again
To endure the unending beat of the air,
Having been nursed beyond the sopping rain,
    Back down the stair.

I called him to come in,
The wide lawn darkened so.
Laughing, he held his chin
And hid beside a bush.
The light gave him a push,
Shadowy grass moved slow.
He crept on agile toes
Under a sheltering rose.

His mother, still beyond
The bare porch and the door,
Called faintly out of sound,
And vanished with her voice.
I caught his curious eyes
Measuring me, and more—
The light dancing behind
My shoulder in the wind.

Then, struck beyond belief
By the child's voice I heard,
I saw his hair turn leaf,
His dancing toes divide
To hooves on either side,
One hand become a bird.
Startled, I held my tongue
To hear what note he sang.

Where was the boy gone now?
I stood on the grass, alone.
Swung from the apple bough
The bees ignored my cry.

A dog roved past, and I
Turned up a sinking stone,
But found beneath no more
Than grasses dead last year.

Suddenly lost and cold,
I knew the yard lay bare.
I longed to touch and hold
My child, my talking child,
Laughing or tame or wild—
Solid in light and air,
The supple hands, the face
To fill that barren place.

Slowly, the leaves descended,
The birds resolved to hands;
Laugh, and the charm was ended,
The hungry boy stepped forth.
He stood on the hard earth,
Like one who understands
Fairy and ghost—but less
Our human loneliness.

Then, on the withering lawn,
He walked beside my arm.
Trees and the sun were gone,
Everything gone but us.
His mother sang in the house,
And kept our supper warm,
And loved us, God knows how,
The wide earth darkened so.

Dog in a Cornfield

Fallow between the horny trees
    The empty field
Lay underneath the motions of the cloud.
My master called for bobwhites on his knees,
    And suddenly the wind revealed
The body pitching forward in the mud.

My master leaped alive at first,
    And cried, and ran
Faster than air could echo feet and hands.
The lazy maples wailed beyond the crust
    Of earth and artificial man.
Here lay one death the autumn understands.

How could I know he ran to lie,
    And joke with me,
Beside the toppled scarecrow there, as though
His body, like the straw, lay beaten dry?
    Growling, I circled near a tree,
Indifferent to a solitary crow.

Down on the stubble field the pair
    Lay side by side,
Scarecrow and master. I could hardly tell
Body from body, and the color of hair
    Blended, to let my master hide.
His laughter thickened like a droning bell.

I called him out of earth, to come
    And walk with me,
To leave that furrow where the man's shape broke,

To let the earth collapse, and come on home.
　　The limber scarecrow knew the way
To meet the wind, that monumental joke;

But once the real man tumbled down,
　　Funny or not,
The broomstick and the straw might leap and cry.
Scared of the chance to wrestle wood and stone,
　　I howled into the air, forgot
How scarecrows stumble in a field to die.

Snarling, I leaped the rusty fence,
　　I ran across
The shock of leaves, blundering as I tore
Into the scarecrow in the man's defense.
　　My master rolled away on grass
And saw me scatter legs and arms in air.

And saw me summon all my force
　　To shake apart
The brittle shoes, the tough blades of the brains
Back to the ground; the brutal formlessness,
　　The twisted knot of its arid heart
Back to the sweet roots of the autumn rains.

Where do the sticks and stones get off,
　　Mocking the shape
Of eyes younger than summer, of thoughtful hands?
The real man falls to nothing fast enough.
　　I barked into the air, to keep
The man quick to a joy he understands.

On Minding One's Own Business

Ignorant two, we glide
On ripples near the shore.
The rainbows leap no more,
And men in boats alight
To see the day subside.

All evening fins have drowned
Back in the summer dark.
Above us, up the bank,
Obscure on lonely ground,
A shack receives the night.

I hold the lefthand oar
Out of the wash, and guide
The skiff away so wide
We wander out of sight
As soundless as before.

We will not land to bear
Our will upon that house,
Nor force on any place
Our dull offensive weight.

Somebody may be there,
Peering at us outside
Across the even lake,
Wondering why we take
Our time and stay so late.

Long may the lovers hide
In viny shacks from those
Who thrash among the trees,
Who curse, who have no peace,

Who pitch and moan all night
For fear of someone's joys,
Deploring the human face.

From prudes and muddying fools,
Kind Aphrodite, spare
All hunted criminals,
Hoboes, and whip-poor-wills,
And girls with rumpled hair,
All, all of whom might hide
Within that darkening shack.
Lovers may live, and abide.
Wherefore, I turn my back,
And trawl our boat away,
Lest someone fear to call
A girl's name till we go
Over the lake so slow
We hear the darkness fall.

The Morality of Poetry
to Gerald Enscoe

Would you the undulation of one wave, its trick to me
    transfer. . . .

—WHITMAN

I stood above the sown and generous sea
Late in the day, to muse about your words:
Your human images come to pray for hands
To wipe their vision clear, your human voice
Flinging the poem forward into sound.
Below me, roaring elegies to birds,
Intricate, cold, the waters crawled the sands,
Heaving and groaning, casting up a tree,
A shell, a can to clamber over the ground:
Slow celebration, cluttering ripple on wave.

I wondered when the complicated sea
Would tear and tangle in itself and die,
Sheer outrage hammering itself to death:
Hundreds of gulls descending to the froth,
Their bodies clumped and fallen, lost to me.
Counting those images, I meant to say
A hundred gulls decline to nothingness;
But, high in cloud, a single naked gull
Shadows a depth in heaven for the eye.
And, for the ear, under the wail and snarl
Of groping foghorns and the winds grown old,
A single human word for love of air
Gathers the tangled discords up to song.
Summon the rare word for the rare desire.
It thrives on hunger, and it rises strong
To live above the blindness and the noise
Only as long as bones are clean and spare,
The spine exactly set, the muscles lean.
Before you let a single word escape,

Starve it in darkness; lash it to the shape
Of tense wing skimming on the sea alone. . . .

So through my cold lucidity of heart
I thought to send you careful rules of song.
But gulls ensnare me here; the sun fades; thought
By thought the tide heaves, bobbing my words' damp
        wings;
Mind is the moon-wave roiling on ripples now.
Sun on the bone-hulled galleons of those gulls
Charms my immense irrelevance away,
And lures wings moonward. Openly she soars,
A miracle out of all gray sounds, the moon,
Deepening and rifting swell and formal sky.
Woman or bird, she plumes the ashening sound,
Flaunting to nothingness the rules I made.
Scattering cinders, widening, over the sand
Her cold epistle falls. To plumb the fall
Of silver on ripple, evening ripple on wave,
Quick celebration where she lives for light,
I let all measures die. My voice is gone,
My words to you unfinished, where they lie
Common and bare as stone in diamond veins.
Where the sea moves the word moves, where the sea
Subsides, the slow word fades with lunar tides.
Now still alive, my skeletal words gone bare,
Lapsing like dead gulls' brittle wings and drowned,
In a mindless dance, beneath the darkening air,
I send you shoreward echoes of my voice:
The dithyrambic gestures of the moon,
Sun-lost, the mind plumed, Dionysian,
A blue sea-poem, joy, moon-ripple on wave.

At the Slackening of the Tide

Today I saw a woman wrapped in rags
Leaping along the beach to curse the sea.
Her child lay floating in the oil, away
From oarlock, gunwale, and the blades of oars.
The skinny lifeguard, raging at the sky,
Vomited sea, and fainted on the sand.

The cold simplicity of evening falls
Dead on my mind,
And underneath the piles the water
Leaps up, leaps up, and sags down slowly, farther
Than seagulls disembodied in the drag
Of oil and foam.

Plucking among the oyster shells a man
Stares at the sea, that stretches on its side.
Now far along the beach, a hungry dog
Announces everything I knew before:
Obliterate naiads weeping underground,
Where Homer's tongue thickens with human howls.

I would do anything to drag myself
Out of this place:
Root up a seaweed from the water,
To stuff it in my mouth, or deafen me,
Free me from all the force of human speech;
Go drown, almost.

Warm in the pleasure of the dawn I came
To sing my song
And look for mollusks in the shallows,
The whorl and coil that pretty up the earth,

While far below us, flaring in the dark,
The stars go out.

What did I do to kill my time today,
After the woman ranted in the cold,
The mellow sea, the sound blown dark as wine?
After the lifeguard rose up from the waves
Like a sea-lizard with the scales washed off?
Sit there, admiring sunlight on a shell?

Abstract with terror of the shell, I stared
Over the waters where
God brooded for the living all one day.
Lonely for weeping, starved for a sound of mourning,
I bowed my head, and heard the sea far off
Washing its hands.

All the Beautiful Are Blameless

Out of a dark into the dark she leaped
Lightly this day.
Heavy with prey, the evening skiffs are gone,
And drowsy divers lift their helmets off,
Dry on the shore.

Two stupid harly-charlies got her drunk
And took her swimming naked on the lake.
The waters rippled lute-like round the boat,
And far beyond them, dipping up and down,
Unmythological sylphs, their names unknown,
Beckoned to sandbars where the evenings fall.

Only another drunk would say she heard
A natural voice
Luring the flesh across the water.
I think of those unmythological
Sylphs of the trees.

Slight but orplidean shoulders weave in dusk
Before my eyes when I walk lonely forward
To kick beer-cans from tracked declivities.
If I, being lightly sane, may carve a mouth
Out of the air to kiss, the drowned girl surely
Listened to lute-song where the sylphs are gone.
The living and the dead glide hand in hand
Under cool waters where the days are gone.
Out of the dark into a dark I stand.

The ugly curse the world and pin my arms
Down by their grinning teeth, sneering a blame.
Closing my eyes, I look for hungry swans

To plunder the lake and bear the girl away,
Back to the larger waters where the sea
Sifts, judges, gathers the body, and subsides.

But here the starved, touristic crowd divides
And offers the dead
Hell for the living body's evil:
The girl flopped in the water like a pig
And drowned dead drunk.

So do the pure defend themselves. But she,
Risen to kiss the sky, her limbs still whole,
Rides on the dark tarpaulin toward the shore;
And the hired saviours turn their painted shell
Along the wharf, to list her human name.
But the dead have no names, they lie so still,
And all the beautiful are blameless now.

There Hugo Wolf is buried: fully formed
Out of the stone a naked woman leans
Kissing the uncut stone, the solid void
Of granite cold to sound and song unmade.
She holds her body to the rock, unwarmed
By any sculptor's trick. The climbing vines
Fail to relieve what barren death destroyed:
The life half over, and the song gone dead.

Somewhere unborn inside the stone a mouth
Hungered severely for her starving kiss.
Reaching his lover's hands across the dark,
Maybe the dead musician underneath
Whispers to touch the woman's nakedness,
To strike a fire inside the yearning rock.

Brush aside that fantasy, I feel
The wind of early autumn cross the ground,
I turn among the stones to let it blow
Clearly across my face as over stone.
Bodiless yearnings make no music fall;
Breath of the body bears the living sound.
This dour musician died so long ago
Even his granite beard is softened down.

An age or so will wear away his grave,
The lover who attains the girl be rain,
The granite underneath be carved no more.
Only the living body calls up love,
That shadow risen casually from stone
To clothe the nakedness of bare desire.

A Prayer in My Sickness
la muerte entra y sale

You hear the long roll of the plunging ground,
The whistle of stones, the quail's cry in the grass.
I stammer like a bird, I rasp like stone,
I mutter, with gray hands upon my face.
The earth blurs, beyond me, into dark.
Spinning in such bewildered sleep, I need
To know you, whirring above me, when I wake.
Come down. Come down. I lie afraid.
I have lain alien in my self so long,
How can I understand love's angry tongue?

I should have been delighted there to hear
The woman and the boy,
Singing along the shore together.
Lightly the shawl and shoulder of the sea
Upbore the plume and body of one gull
Dropping his lines.

Loping behind a stone too large for waves
To welter down like pumice without sound,
Laughing his languages awake, that boy
Flung to his mother, on a wrack of weeds,
Delicate words, a whisper like a spume
Fluting along the edges of the shore.

I should have been delighted that the cries
Of fishermen and gulls
Faded among the swells, to let me
Gather into the fine seines of my ears
The frail fins of their voices as they sang:
My wife and child.

Lovely the mother shook her hair, so long
And glittering in its darkness, as the moon
In the deep lily-heart of the hollowing swells
Flamed toward the cold caves of the evening sea:
And the fine living frieze of her Greek face;
The sea behind her, fading, and the sails.

I should have been delighted for the gaze,
The billowing of the girl,
The bodying skirt, the ribbons falling;
I should have run to gather in my arms
The mother and the child who seemed to live
Stronger than stone and wave.

But slowly twilight gathered up the skiffs
Into its long gray arms; and though the sea
Grew kind as possible to wrack-splayed birds;
And though the sea like woman vaguely wept;
She could not hide her clear enduring face,
Her cold divinities of death and change.

Stress of his anger set me back
To musing over time and space.
The apple branches dripping black
Divided light across his face.
Towering beneath the broken tree,
He seemed a stony shade to me.
He spoke no language I could hear
For long with my distracted ear.

Between his lips and my delight
In blowing wind, a bird-song rose.
And soon in fierce, blockading light
The planet's shadow hid his face.
And all that strongly molded bone
Of chest and shoulder soon were gone,
Devoured among the solid shade.
Assured his angry voice was dead,

And satisfied his judging eyes
Had given over plaguing me,
I stood to let the darkness rise—
My darkness, gathering in the tree,
The field, the swollen shock of hay,
Bank of the creek half washed away.
Lost in my self, and unaware
Of love, I took the evening air.

I blighted, for a moment's length,
My father out of sight and sound;
Prayed to annihilate his strength,
The proud legs planted on the ground.

Why should I hear his angry cry
Or bear the damning of his eye?
Anger for anger I could give,
And murder for my right to live.

The moon rose. Lucidly the moon
Ran skimming shadows off the trees,
To strip all shadow but its own
Down to the perfect mindlessness.
Yet suddenly the moonlight caught
My father's fingers reaching out,
The strong arm begging me for love,
Loneliness I knew nothing of.

And weeping in the nakedness
Of moonlight and of agony,
His blue eyes lost their barrenness
And bore a blossom out to me.
And as I ran to give it back,
The apple branches, dripping black,
Trembled across the lunar air
And dropped white petals on his hair.

A Winter Day in Ohio

P. W. T. died in late Spring, 1957

Clever, defensive, seasoned animals
Plato and Christ deny your grave. But man,
Who slept for years alone, will turn his face
Alone to the common wall before his time.
Between the woodchuck and the cross, alone
All afternoon, I take my time to mourn.
I am too cold to cry against the snow
Of roots and stars, drifting above your face.

II. A Sequence of Love Poems

Thou know'st, the first time that we smell the air
We wawl and cry.

—King Lear

A Breath of Air

I walked, when love was gone,
Out of the human town,
For an easy breath of air.
Beyond a break in the trees,
Beyond the hangdog lives
Of old men, beyond girls:
The tall stars held their peace.
Looking in vain for lies
I turned, like earth, to go.
An owl's wings hovered, bare
On the moon's hills of snow.

And things were as they were.

In Shame and Humiliation

He will launch a curse upon the world, and as only man can curse (it is his privilege, the primary distinction between him and other animals), maybe by his curse alone he will attain his object—that is, convince himself that he is a man and not a piano-key!   —DOSTOYEVSKY, *Notes from Underground*

What can a man do that a beast cannot,
A bird, a reptile, any fiercer thing?
> He can amaze the ground
With anger never hissed in a snake's throat
> Or past a bitch's fang,
Though, suffocate, he cannot make a sound.

He can out-rage the forked tongue with a word,
The iron forged of his pain, over and over,
> Till the cold blade can fall
And beak an enemy's heart quick as a bird,
> And then retire to cover,
To vines of hair, declivities of skull.

Outright the snake, faster than man, can kill.
A mongrel's teeth can snarl as man's cannot.
> And a bird, unbodied soul
Soaring and dazzling, in the cloud at will
> Outbeautifies the flight
Of halt man's clavicles that flop and wheel.

Their cries last longer. Sinew of wing and coil,
Or sprung thighs of hounds impinge their iron
> Easy and quick, to leap
Over the brooks, the miles and days, like oil
> Flung on a surge of green.
A man limps into nothing more than sleep.

But under the dream he always dreams too late,
That stark abounding dream of wretchedness
    Where stones and very trees
Ignore his name, and crows humiliate,
    And fiends below the face,
Serpents, women, and dogs dance to deny his face—

He will not deny, he will not deny his own.
Thrashing in lakes or pools of broken glass,
    He hunches over to look
And feel his mouth, his nostrils, feel of the bone,
    A man's ultimate face:
The individual bone, that burns like ice.

That fire, that searing cold is what I claim:
What makes me man, that dogs can never share,
    Woman or brilliant bird,
The beaks that mock but cannot speak the names
    Of the blind rocks, of the stars.
Sprawling in dark, I burn my sudden pride.

Let my veins wither now, my words revolt
Serpent or bird or pure untroubled mind.
    I will avow my face
Unto my face and, through the spirit's **vault**,
    Deliberate underground,
Devour the locusts of my bitterness.

That angel, wheeled upon my heart, **survives**,
Nourished by food the righteous cannot eat
    And loathe to move among.
They die, fastidious, while the spirit thrives
    Out of its own defeat.
The pure, the pure! will never live so long.

I kissed you in the dead of dark,
And no one knew, or wished to know,
You bore, across your face, a mark
From birth, those shattered years ago.
Now I can never keep in mind
The memory of your ugliness
At a clear moment. Now my blind
Fingers alone can read your face.

Often enough I had seen that slash
Of fire you quickly hid in shame;
You flung your scarf across the flesh,
And turned away, and said my name.
Thus I remember daylight and
The scar that made me pity you.
God damn them both, you understand.
Pity can scar love's face, I know.

I loved your face because your face
Was broken. When my hands were heavy,
You kissed me only in a darkness
To make me daydream you were lovely.
All the lovely emptiness
On earth is easy enough to find.
You had no right to turn your face
From me. Only the truth is kind.

I cannot dream of you by night.
I half-remember what you were.
And I remember the cold daylight,
And pity your disgusting scar

As any light-eyed fool could pity,
Who sees you walking down the street.
I lose your stark essential beauty,
I dream some face I read about.

If I were given a blind god's power
To turn your daylight on again,
I would not raise you smooth and pure:
I would bare to heaven your uncommon pain,
Your scar I had a right to hold,
To look on, for the pain was yours.
Now you are dead, and I grow old,
And the doves cackle out of doors,

And lovers, flicking on the lights,
Turn to behold each lovely other.
Let them remember fair delights.
How can I ever love another?
You had no right to banish me
From that scarred truth of wretchedness,
Your face, that I shall never see
Again, though I search every place.

I cannot live nor die.
Now shadows rise nor fall,
Whisper aloud nor weep.
Struck beyond time and change
To a claw, a withering thigh,
A breath, a slackening call
To cold throats out of range,
I fade to a broken hope.

What good may mourning do,
The sigh, the soft lament,
The poised turning away
To name one faded name?
I will not name it now.
The day, the heart lie spent.
I find, now that I came,
Love that I cannot say.

The wind builds hock and tongue
Up from the sinewy ground.
But how may the blind air tell
A gnat from a lark? Alone,
Weighed by the laboring sound
Of wind on muscle and hair,
White as a thistle and bare,
I close the gate of hell.

Neat, shallow, hell is here,
Here, where I speak to lips
At one with stone and me,
Living and dead at one:

Love's cry, the shock of fear,
The shadow of rain that drips,
A mirror of gleaming stone,
The hands that cannot see,

Ears stricken blind, and eyes
That cannot speak nor sing,
And arms that barely breathe
Above ground or below.
Lumbering from hell, I gaze
Down at the earth so long,
I need no further go.
Here is the gate of wreath.

Love need no further go
Than back to the earth, to die.
The living need not seek
For love but underfoot.
The first star rises slow
And brambles lash my eye
And lichens trip my foot,
And yet, I cannot speak.

I will stand here, till dawn.
I will not fall down, to pray.
Dark bells may summon you
Out of your dream to cry.
Then I will tread your lawn
Through a soft break of day,
To see your day go by,
Who stare, and stare me through.

When I came back from my last dream, when I
Whirled in the morning snowfall up the lawn,
I looked behind me where my wings were gone.
Rusting above the snow, for lack of care,
A pile of rakes and shovels rotted away.
Tools of the world were crumbling into air,
And I, neither the living nor the dead,
Paused in the dusk of dawn to wonder why
Any man clambers upward out of shade
To rake and shovel all his dust away.

I found my body sprawled against the bed.
One hand flopped back as though to ward away
Shovels of light. The body wakes to burial;
But my face rebelled; the lids and lips were gray,
And spiders climbed their webs above my head.
I stood above my wreck of flesh and skull:
A foot reclined over the wrenching thigh,
And suddenly, before I joined my face,
The eyelids opened, and it stared across
The window pane, into the empty sky.

Neither the living nor the dead I stood,
Longing to leave my poor flesh huddled there
Heaped up for burning under the last laments.
I moved, to leap on spider webs and climb.
But where do spiders fling those filaments,
Those pure formalities of blood and air,
Both perfect and alive? I did no good.
The hands of daylight hammered down my ghost,
And I was home now, bowing into my dust,
To quicken into stupor one more time,
One of the living buried like the dead.

40

A Girl Walking into a Shadow

The mere trees cast no coolness where you go.
Your small feet press no darkness into the grass.
I know your weight of days, and mourn I know.
All hues beneath the ground are bare grayness.

When I was young, I might have touched your hair,
Gestured my warning, how that fire will gray,
Slight arms and delicate hands fall heavier,
And pale feet hasten to a dark delay.

Now old, I love you slowly, through my sound.
Lightly alive, you cannot mourn for trees.
You cannot care how grass, above the ground,
Gathers to mold your shadow's quick caress.

Heavy for you, I hear the futile speech
Of air in trees, of shadows in your hair.
Quick to go by me now, beyond my reach,
You pause. With darkness deepening everywhere,

Something of light falls, pitiful and kind.
Something of love forgot the dark embrace
Of evening, where the lover's eyes go blind
With dreaming on the hollows of your face.

I dreamed that I was dead, as all men do,
And feared the dream, though hardly for the sake
Of any thrust of pain my flesh might take
Below the softening shales. Bereft of you,
I lay for days and days alone, I knew
Somewhere above me boughs were burning gold,
And women's frocks were loose, and men grew old.

Grew old. And shrivelled. Asked the time of day.
And then forgot. Turned. Looked among the grass.
Tripped on a twig. Frightened some leaves away.
Children. And girls. I knew, above my face,
Rabbit and jay flocked, wondering how to cross
An empty field stripped naked to the sun.
They halted into a shadow, huddled down.

Rabbit and jay, old man, and girl, and child,
All moved above me, dreaming of broad light.
I heard you walking through the empty field.
Startled awake, I found my living sight:
The grave drifted away, and it was night,
I felt your soft despondent shoulders near.
Out of my dream, the dead rose everywhere.

I did not dream your death, but only mine.

III. The Part Nearest Home

From the uttermost part of the earth have we heard songs,
even glory to the righteous. But I said, My leanness, my
leanness, woe unto me.

—Isaiah, 24:16

What the Earth Asked Me

"Why did you kiss the girl who cried
For lovers through her lonely mind,
Homely as sin and sick of pride?"

   In pity for my kind.

"What good will pity do the lost
Who flutter in the driven wind,
Wild for the body, ghost on ghost?"

   No good, no good to me.

"Why did you hammer with your fist
That beetle on the window-blind,
Withered in summer's holocaust?"

   In pity for my kind.

"What good will pity do the found
Who flutter in the driven wind,
Wild to be ghosts below the ground?"

   No good, no good to me.

"The living and the dead together
Flutter before, flutter behind.
Why do you try to change the weather?"

   In pity for my kind.

"What good will pity do the kiss
That shrivels on the mouth of grief?
Have you been calling me for this?"

   No good to me, no good to me.

The Refusal

When we get back, the wagon will be gone,
The porchlight empty in the wind, no doubt;
    And everybody here,
Who damned us for the conscience of a stone,
    Will tell us to get out
And do our sniffling in the dark somewhere.

It may not be delight to hear that word,
The pride of mourners mocking in our faces.
    I offer no delight,
Neither a soft life, nor a grave deferred.
    I have known other places
Ugly as this, and shut them from my sight.

Inside the house, somebody we could love,
Who labored for us till the taut string gave,
    Stares from a half-closed eye.
Why should we gaze back in that pit of love?
    All the beloved lie
In the perpetual savagery of graves.

Come here to me; I will not let you go
To suffer on some relative's hard shoulder—
    Weeping woman or man.
God, I have died so many days ago,
    The funeral began
When I was born, and will go on forever:—

Unless I shut the door myself, and take
Your elbow, drag you bodily, out of breath
    And let the house grow dark.

46

Inside, that lamentation for the sake
     Of numbers on a rock
Starves me and freezes you, and kills us both.

Must we reel with the wine of mourning like a drunk?
Look there, the doors are latched, the windows close,
     And we are told to go.
When we come back, the granite will be sunk
     An inch or more below
The careful fingers of the healing snows.

Preacher and undertaker follow the cars;
They claimed the comfort of the earth, and lied.
     Better to trust the moon
Blown in the soft bewilderment of stars;
     The living lean on pain,
The hard stones of the earth are on our side.

American Twilights, 1957

to Caryl Chessman

1

The buckles glitter, billies lean
Supple and cold as men on walls.
The trusties' faces, yawning green,
Summon up heart, as someone calls
For light, for light! and evening falls.

Checking the cells, the warden piles
Shadow on shadow where he goes
Beyond the catwalk, down the files,
Sneering at one who thumbs his nose.
One weeps, and stumbles on his toes.

Tear and tormented snicker and heart
Click in the darkness; close, and fade.
Clean locks together mesh and part,
And lonely lifers, foot and head,
Huddle against the bed they made.

2

Lie dark, beloved country, now.
Trouble no dream, so still you lie.
Citizens drawl their dreams away;
Stupored, they hid their agony
Deep in the rock; but men must die.

Tall on the earth I would have sung
Heroes of hell, could I have learned
Their names to marvel on my tongue;

The land is dark where they have turned,
And now their very names are burned.

But buried under trestled rock
The broken thief and killer quake:
Tower by tower and clock by clock
Citizens wind the towns asleep.
God, God have pity when they wake.

Haunted by gallows, peering in dark,
I conjure prisons out of wet
And strangling pillows where I mark
The misery man must not forget,
Though I have found no prison yet.

Lo now, the desolation man
Has tossed away like a gnawed bone
Will hunt him where the sea began,
Summon him out of tree and stone,
Damn him, before his dream be gone:—

Seek him behind his bars, to crack
Out the dried kernel of his heart.
God, God have pity if he wake,
Have mercy on man who dreamed apart.
God, God have pity on man apart.

I longed to kill you once, when I was young,
Because you laughed at me before my friends.
        And now the baffled prose
Of a belated vengeance numbs my tongue.
        Come back, before the last wind bends
Your body to the void beyond repose.

Standing alone before your grave, I read
The name, the season, every decent praise
        A chisel might devise—
Deliberate scrawls to guard us from the dead.
        And yet I lift my strength, to raise
Out of the mossy wallow your pig's eyes.

The summons fell, but I could not come home
To gloat above the hacking and the rasp
        Caught in your corded throat;
And, many towns away, I heard your doom
        Tolling the hate beyond my grasp,
Thieving the poisons of my angry thought.

After so many years to lose the vision
Of your last anguish! Furious at the cheat,
        After your burial
I traveled here, to lay my weak derision
        Fresh as a garland at your feet.
All day I have gathered curses, but they fail.

I cannot even call to mind so clearly,
As once I could, your confident thin voice
        Banishing me to nothing.

Your hand crumbles, your sniffing nostrils barely
      Evoke the muscles of my loathing;
And I too die, who came here to rejoice.

Lost mocker of my childhood, how the moss
Softens your lair, how deeply nibbling fangs
      Sink in the careless ground.
Seasons of healing grasses weave across
      Your caving lips, and dull my strange
Terror of failures. Shaken, I have found

Nothing to mark you off in earth but stone.
Walking here lonely and strange now, I must find
      A grave to prod my wrath
Back to its just devotions. Miserable bone,
      Devouring jaw-hinge, glare gone blind,
Come back, be damned of me, your aftermath.

At the Executed Murderer's Grave
(for J. L. D.)

*Why should we do this? What good is it to us? Above all, how
can we do such a thing? How can it possibly be done?*

—FREUD

1

My name is James A. Wright, and I was born
Twenty-five miles from this infected grave,
In Martins Ferry, Ohio, where one slave
To Hazel-Atlas Glass became my father.
He tried to teach me kindness. I return
Only in memory now, aloof, unhurried,
To dead Ohio, where I might lie buried,
Had I not run away before my time.
Ohio caught George Doty. Clean as lime,
His skull rots empty here. Dying's the best
Of all the arts men learn in a dead place.
I walked here once. I made my loud display,
Leaning for language on a dead man's voice.
Now sick of lies, I turn to face the past.
I add my easy grievance to the rest:

2

Doty, if I confess I do not love you,
Will you let me alone? I burn for my own lies.
The nights electrocute my fugitive,
My mind. I run like the bewildered mad
At St. Clair Sanitarium, who lurk,
Arch and cunning, under the maple trees,
Pleased to be playing guilty after dark.

Staring to bed, they croon self-lullabies.
Doty, you make me sick. I am not dead.
I croon my tears at fifty cents per line.

3

Idiot, he demanded love from girls,
And murdered one. Also, he was a thief.
He left two women, and a ghost with child.
The hair, foul as a dog's upon his head,
Made such revolting Ohio animals
Fitter for vomit than a kind man's grief.
I waste no pity on the dead that stink,
And no love's lost between me and the crying
Drunks of Belaire, Ohio, where police
Kick at their kidneys till they die of drink.
Christ may restore them whole, for all of me.
Alive and dead, those giggling muckers who
Saddled my nightmares thirty years ago
Can do without my widely printed sighing
Over their pains with paid sincerity.
I do not pity the dead, I pity the dying.

4

I pity myself, because a man is dead.
If Belmont County killed him, what of me?
His victims never loved him. Why should we?
And yet, nobody had to kill him either.
It does no good to woo the grass, to veil
The quicklime hole of a man's defeat and shame.

Nature-lovers are gone. To hell with them.
I kick the clods away, and speak my name.

5

This grave's gash festers. Maybe it will heal,
When all are caught with what they had to do
In fear of love, when every man stands still
By the last sea,
And the princes of the sea come down
To lay away their robes, to judge the earth
And its dead, and we dead stand undefended everywhere,
And my bodies—father and child and unskilled crim-
       inal—
Ridiculously kneel to bare my scars,
My sneaking crimes, to God's unpitying stars.

6

Staring politely, they will not mark my face
From any murderer's, buried in this place.
Why should they? We are nothing but a man.

7

Doty, the rapist and the murderer,
Sleeps in a ditch of fire, and cannot hear;
And where, in earth or hell's unholy peace,
Men's suicides will stop, God knows, not I.
Angels and pebbles mock me under trees.
Earth is a door I cannot even face.
Order be damned, I do not want to die,

Even to keep Belaire, Ohio, safe.
The hackles on my neck are fear, not grief.
(Open, dungeon! Open, roof of the ground!)
I hear the last sea in the Ohio grass,
Heaving a tide of gray disastrousness.
Wrinkles of winter ditch the rotted face
Of Doty, killer, imbecile, and thief:
Dirt of my flesh, defeated, underground.

When I went out to kill myself, I caught
A pack of hoodlums beating up a man.
Running to spare his suffering, I forgot
My name, my number, how my day began,
How soldiers milled around the garden stone
And sang amusing songs; how all that day
Their javelins measured crowds; how I alone
Bargained the proper coins, and slipped away.

Banished from heaven, I found this victim beaten,
Stripped, kneed, and left to cry. Dropping my rope
Aside, I ran, ignored the uniforms:
Then I remembered bread my flesh had eaten,
The kiss that ate my flesh. Flayed without hope,
I held the man for nothing in my arms.